Key West.

Literary Sands of Key West

Also in this series:

LITERARY
SANDS
OF
KEY WEST

by Patricia Altobello
and Deirdre Pierce

Illustrated by Nela J. Benavides

STARRHILL PRESS
Washington, D.C.

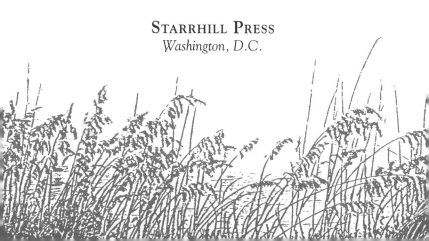

*For Linda Donald, our own personal angel
who left the party too soon.*

And, ever and always, for Roundy.

Designed by Gibson Parsons Design
Edited by Elizabeth Brown Lockman and Paige Meginley
Text copyright © 1996 by Patricia Altobello and Deirdre Pierce
All rights reserved.
Illustrations by Nela J. Benavides
Hand-marbled paper by Iris Nevins, Sussex, New Jersey
Printed in the United States of America
Copyright © 1996 by Starrhill Press. All rights reserved.
This book, or any portions thereof, may not be reproduced in any form
without written permission of the publisher.

Any inquiries should be directed to Starrhill Press, P.O. Box 21038,
Washington, DC 20009-0538, telephone (202) 387-9805.

8 7 6 5 4 3 2 1   1996 1997 1998 1999 2000 2001 2002 2003

Library of Congress Cataloging-in-Publication Data

Altobello, Patricia.
        The literary sands of Key West / by Patricia Altobello and Deirdre Pierce.
        p.   cm.
        Includes index.
        ISBN 1-57359-004-5 (alk. paper)
        1. Authors, American—Homes and haunts—Florida—Key West—
    Guidebooks. 2. American literature—Florida—Key West—History and
    criticism. 3. Literary landmarks—Florida—Key West—Guidebooks.
    4. Walking—Florida—Key West—Guidebooks. 5. Key West (Fla.)—
    Intellectual life. 6. Key West (Fla.)—In literature. I. Pierce, Deirdre. II. Title.
    PS267.K49A48   1996
    810.9'975941—dc20   95-26357
                                                            CIP

Contents

Introduction

Key West is only a big rock, really—a calcified chunk of coral. But it has always had a pull as strong as a magnet in an iron mine. From the beginning, Key West citizens have been the kind of people who like to go to the edge: writers, artists, and rogues. Maybe that's because it's the southernmost point in the continental United States—the last frontier going south. There's a rough-and-tumble feel to the place even today. What's more, the island still has a tolerance inherent in its culture that naturally attracts eccentrics and creative types. So it continues to draw writers to its glorious subtropical gardens, brilliant aqua waters, and summer weather year-round.

Recent Key West bylines have included Thomas Sanchez, whose *Mile Zero* may eventually be judged the definitive Key West novel; biographer and one-time Jack Kerouac editor Ellis Amburn; novelists Peter Taylor, Wilfrid Sheed, Ralph Ellison, Jim Harrison, Robert Stone, and Irving Weinman; inspiring editors like *Esquire*'s fiction chief Rust Hills and *Shenandoah Magazine*'s James Boatwright; and simpatico agents like Dick Duane.

Key West has enticed publishers, too, like Ross Claiborne, Bill Grose, Frank Taylor, and Joan and Wright Langley. There are journalists as well, such as Jane O'Reilly, Barbara Ehrenreich, and Alexander Cockburn.

A long list of nonfiction bestsellers includes Jean Carper with *The Food Pharmacy* and *Food Your Miracle Medicine*; Leigh Rutledge with *A Cat's Little Instruction Book* and *Dear Tabby*; and Nancy Friday with *My Mother/My Self*, *Women on Top*, and *Men in Love*. Key West can also claim prized children's authors like Shel Silverstein and *Babar*'s de Brunhoff family.

Perhaps the main reason contemporary authors flock to Key West is because the island in the Gulf Stream is well out of the mainstream. It's far away from A-list book tour pressures and social posturing for critical acclaim. There's no Elaine's, no Algonquin Round Table—nothing even close. There are plenty of writers' haunts in Key West, but little writers' flaunt.

The easygoing attitude of the island is infectious. The friendly Conchs, as the locals are called, are delighted to share their paradise with all comers. They are proud of the fact that Key West is all kinds of things to all kinds of people. It's gay and straight. It's chic and funky. It's rich and famous. It's down and out. And, best of all, it is dripping with literary history. Both past and present, Key West has a very literary soul. So pack some comfortable footgear or pull up a familiar footstool and sift through the literary sands that make Key West a favorite destination for inveterate readers.

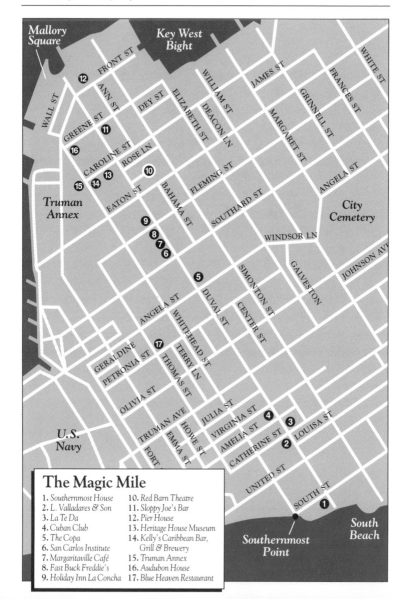

The Magic Mile

1. *Southernmost House*
2. *L. Valladares & Son*
3. *La Te Da*
4. *Cuban Club*
5. *The Copa*
6. *San Carlos Institute*
7. *Margaritaville Café*
8. *Fast Buck Freddie's*
9. *Holiday Inn La Concha*
10. *Red Barn Theatre*
11. *Sloppy Joe's Bar*
12. *Pier House*
13. *Heritage House Museum*
14. *Kelly's Caribbean Bar, Grill & Brewery*
15. *Truman Annex*
16. *Audubon House*
17. *Blue Heaven Restaurant*

The Magic Mile

Just over one mile separates the Gulf of Mexico from the Atlantic Ocean in the heart of Key West's Old Town neighborhood. It's the kind of geographic oddity that instantly marks the downtown as exceptional. Go from sea to shining sea in 20 minutes at a moderate pace, or stroll in the languid mode so familiar to natives. A further cue from resident sages mandates a hat in the months of April through October.

Duval Street populated by boutiques, galleries, restaurants, and guesthouses marks the straight line between the two oceans. Start at the Atlantic end of Duval, lately referred to as the "upscale end of town." Right on the ocean is a glorious brick Victorian known as the **Southernmost House** (1400 Duval St.), all pink-and-aqua trim with an air of family secrets about it. Built for a leading judge around 1900 and officially named the J. Vining Harris House, it was later a popular restaurant, Casa Cayo Hueso, where glitterati of the 1940s and 1950s often dined. No less a duo than Carson McCullers and Tennessee Williams shared a table there in its prime. A private house now, the turreted, gabled, and geegawed giant is an example of the Queen Anne Victorian style taken to the tropics.

When it was located at 517 Fleming Street, **L. Valladares & Son** (1200 Duval St.) was a regular check-in on Ernest Hemingway's schedule. The newsstand today is run by Arthur Valladares, who still remembers the first time he saw the husky author. It was in 1928 when the writer came in to place signed copies of *The Sun Also Rises* with Leonte Valladares, Arthur's father. To the young boy, the ill-dressed Hemingway looked like any other ragtag ne'er-do-well. The child, in fact, fetched his father with the report that a poor man had come in for their help. Today, the store's vast selection of literary and poetry reviews and huge inventory of foreign magazines

Southernmost House

makes it the ultimate for press mavens.

The white balconied building at 1125 Duval Street became known as La Terrazza Da Martí after the Cuban revolutionary poet José Martí delivered a rousing call from the Duval Street overhang in 1894 to raise funds for Cuba's budding revolution against Spain. Called the George Washington of Cuba, Martí was a journalist as well, filing dispatches for the New York and Central American newspapers.

Now, **La Te Da** (for LA TErrazza DA Martí) is a particularly pleasant restaurant and a tropical entertainment complex, too. Its inviting open barroom and fountained swimming pool are the enticements that have made La Te Da a local institution for years. Even if one doesn't choose to dine here, a side trip to La Te Da in the calm of the afternoon is in order just to see the wall full of original Picasso prints from the owner's collection. There is something intellectually splendid about having a quiet drink just a nose-length away from an abundance of Picassos.

Sunday tea dances, holiday theme extravaganzas, occasional drag pageants, and more make the restaurant a center for the night people who comprise today's Key West demimonde. It's the place Tennessee Williams might have frequented to soak up some of the late-night characters as fodder for his fictional profiles. The piano lasts until one in the morning; the cast of characters until four.

Diagonally across Duval from La Te Da at 1102 is the stylish-looking 1920s **Cuban Club**. Called the Sociedad Cuba, it was the hub of Cuban life when Ernest Hemingway was a regular at the weekly cockfights there. Like the bullfights Hemingway was writing about in his Key West studio for *Death in the Afternoon*, the rooster battles that began at high noon on Sundays fascinated the sporting author. These cockfights had been declared illegal by the time the club was destroyed by fire in 1983. Saved from the rubble, however, were the original posts and turrets which, refurbished, grace the two-story reconstruction that currently houses shops and vacation suites.

It is difficult to imagine what Thomas Edison would make of **The Copa** (623 Duval St.), a gay disco now housed in his favorite movie theater, The Monroe. Stationed in Key West during World War I to work on highly secret depth-charge experiments for the Navy, the wizard of electricity loved movies. Local newspapers reported that Edison never missed one night at the flickers during his six-month stay in 1917. (The inventor later settled in Fort Myers, Florida, where a fascinating museum in his former residence includes some of his writings.)

The Copa's pink-and-white movie-palace facade still incorporates the old ticket window. What comes with the price of admission today is a garden bar where talented and attractive female impersonators entertain, a pulsing dance floor with guest DJs, and a stage for frequent concerts with out-of-town musical talent. The myriad features of The Copa also attract a sophisticated, urban-minded band of nongay residents and vacationers who use the club for late-night dancing. They mingle easily with the predominantly gay clientele (and vice versa) and rarely venture into The Copa's more risqué reaches upstairs, which include a video room, male strippers, and private dancers.

The **San Carlos Institute** (516 Duval St.), which opened in 1992 after years of historic restoration, is the site of the annual Key West Literary Seminar. In its 14th year, the seminar attracts the big names in American literature, journalism, and theater. A focal point for the Cuban exile community in the 1890s, the San Carlos was one of the nation's first bilingual schools. Transformed now into an

art gallery, theater, and museum of Cuban culture, the Hispanic-baroque-style building is slated to be the repository of a library on Cuba's influence upon the Florida Keys. A look at the marble staircase and wonderful mosaics fashioned of majolica tiles recalls the

San Carlos Institute

golden days of the San Carlos in the first two decades of this century, when its opera house hosted the best companies on the international circuit—even prima ballerina Pavlova danced there with the Russian Ballet in 1915.

To a whole segment of American youth, **Margaritaville Café** (500 Duval St.) is as much a shrine as any of the sites of Hemingway worship. Ever since the 1970s, when **JIMMY BUFFETT** (1946–) rocked into American pop music culture with lyrics about a tropical-paradise state of mind, thousands have made a pilgrimage to Key West for the sole purpose of being "wasted away again in Margaritaville, looking for my lost shaker of salt."

The singer, who has also championed a fund to save the manatee, Florida's endangered sea cow, still has a house on one of the canals out by the mangrove preserves. Occasionally, he even drops by his bar to sit in for a song or two. Just the thought of catching a glimpse of Buffett keeps the casual café full of "parrot-heads"—as his followers are known—in an agreeable state of buzz throughout the day and night.

Himself the author of four books including *Tales from Margarita-ville* and *Where Is Joe Merchant?*, Buffett is also the inspiration for Mark Humphrey's pop history of Key West, *The Jimmy Buffett Scrapbook*, which presents a fun romp through the hazy heyday of the island's dropout decade. The gregarious songwriter counted among his circle some of the leading writers of 1970s Key West, including Tom McGuane who wrote *Ninety-Two in the Shade* and *The Missouri Breaks* and who eventually married Buffett's sister Laurie.

In the shop adjacent to the Margaritaville Café, the works of Buffett's Key West writing cronies are well represented along with his own signed books and a good mix of Margaritaville memorabilia. Buffett humor is represented by a sign at the store's checkout: "Shoplifters will be bound, gagged, and forced to listen to Barry Manilow."

The Kress 5 and 10 Cent Store cornered the town's retail market—literally—at the junction of Duval and Fleming for 50 years. Ernest Hemingway refers to the "big dime store" in his description of Main Street in *To Have and Have Not*, his 1937 novel whose setting is based on Key West. In 1978 the big dime store was turned into a big-time store—the island's answer to Bloomingdale's. Two local entrepreneurs converted the former Kress Building into the fabulous **Fast Buck Freddie's**, a hip emporium of sleek marketing. Fast Buck's even garnered international attention when the BBC featured the pop marketplace in a 1980s documentary.

Tennessee Williams moved into the **Hotel La Concha** (now Holiday Inn La Concha) at 430 Duval Street in 1947 with his grandfather Walter Dakin because his favorite relative loved hotel living. The locale apparently agreed with Williams, too. He made the final revisions there on *A Streetcar Named Desire*, which was published later that year. Before moving out in 1949, the prolific playwright also wrote *Summer and Smoke* in his sixth-floor room.

The six-story, pink stucco La Concha has been a destination for visiting swells since the late 1920s, when Ernest Hemingway recommended it to his New York editor and other publishing acquaintances. Aspiring novelists can still check into the Tennessee Williams Suite or the Hemingway Suite, the original hotel's only two suites, which were preserved in a 1980s renovation and re-named for the literary giants. Be sure to check out **The Top**, a roof-deck bar with a phenomenal 360-degree panorama that is especially spectacular for sunset-sighting.

Behind 319 Duval Street, which houses the Key West Women's Club, is the **Red Barn Theatre**. Originally a shelter for the transportation necessities of the horse-and-carriage era, the barn became headquarters for the Key West Community Players in the 1940s. Tennessee Williams saw two of his one-act plays staged in this intimate theater during the company's earliest seasons. In the past few years, such nationally known writers as Shel Silverstein and Philip Burton, both Key Westers, have followed the Williams try-out tradition by mounting their new works on the well-worn stage.

Number 200 Duval Street has held a certain stature in literary annals since 1937, when the eponymous Joe Russell moved **Sloppy Joe's Bar** from around the corner at 428 Greene Street (where Captain Tony's is now) with the blessing of his most famous patron, Ernest Hemingway. A natural habitat for writers, the boisterous bar has hosted Tennessee Williams, Gore Vidal, John Dos Passos, Archibald MacLeish, Christopher Isherwood, and hundreds more.

The first of the contemporary luxury hotels built on the island, the **Pier House** (One Duval Street) is woven tightly into the literary fabric of Key West. No less distinguished a talent than Truman Capote lived in a trailer on the hotel's construction site. Tennessee Williams spent long afternoons on the resort's pocket beach and became a fixture in owner David Wolkowsky's life. So friendly were the dramatist and developer that Wolkowsky was among those chosen to be pallbearers at Williams' 1981 funeral.

With an incomparable position on the last few yards of sand before North America turns into the Gulf of Mexico, the Pier House's dining room and bars literally range out over the water. It is no wonder that into its third decade, the Pier House is still a magnet for literary magnates. In the 1950s, the Pier House pilings held up the Havana docks where the *City of Key West* ferry shuttled passengers and their cars to and from Cuba. *Havana*, the 1989 Robert Redford-Raoul Julia film about the revolutionary turmoil in 1958

Shrimp boats

Cuba, used a Hollywood version of this same ferry but did film some beach scenes on location in Key West.

To walk the Magic Mile in reverse and return to the Atlantic, leave the Pier House on the Duval Street side. Bypass Front Street on the immediate right. It's the honky-tonk heart of Key West, with too much tourist bait crammed into the old waterfront area. Instead, walk the three short blocks down Duval to Caroline Street and head west toward the lofty shade trees that signal Whitehead Street a block away. At 410 Caroline, drop in on the **Robert Frost Cottage** tucked behind the **Heritage House Museum**. The tour of Heritage House, a lovely antique-filled manse built in the 1830s, includes a stop in the garden, where guests can listen to original recordings of Frost reading from his own works. The New England bard had already won the Pulitzer by the time he first wintered in Key West in 1934. More than a dozen visits were to follow.

The museum and cottage are now in the hands of the daughter of Jessie Porter Newton, the erudite local historian who befriended Frost. Heritage House hosts weekly poetry readings open for public participation on a drop-in basis and week-long poetry workshops, which attract amateur poets from around the country. One of the treasures of Heritage House is a handwritten copy of "The Gift Outright," the poem Frost recited at the 1961 Kennedy inaugural. The poet gave the poem to Jessie Porter Newton in thanks, he said, for so many worthwhile days in Key West.

Next door on the property that wraps around to Whitehead is the original Pan American Airways House (301 Whitehead St.). In 1928 the fledgling airline inaugurated its service with the United States' first commercial international flight: to Cuba 90 miles away. The airy terraces and gardens now house **Kelly's Caribbean Bar, Grill & Brewery**, owned by actress Kelly McGillis, who made Key West her new hometown a few years back.

Yet to make a professional appearance at one of Key West's

playhouses, McGillis can be seen frequently at the restaurant where she and her husband have installed a microbrewery. Behind a huge glass wall in the main garden, the gleaming brew tanks provide a kind of theater for the observant diner. The McGillis family's local thespian role is currently filled by mother Joan, an active director on the area theater scene where locals wait to see if she can lure her daughter onto the stage.

Across the street are the impressive Presidential Gates, the ironwork entrance to the **Truman Annex**. This 44-acre waterfront residential area features Harry Truman's **Little White House**, recently opened as a museum. The house was part of the naval station when President Truman designated it his winter office in the late 1940s. Its collection includes writings, logs, official documents, and correspondence from the chief executive's ten visits to Key West. Among these is a 1949 letter from Truman to his wife Bess in which he wrote, "I've a notion to move the capital to Key West and just stay."

Presidential missives and musings aside, the most evocative piece in the museum is the fine mahogany poker table where Truman played with some of the leading journalists and authors of the era. John Hersey, the Nobel Prize-winning novelist, painted a rich and charming portrait of Truman in *Key West Tales*, set at the Little White House poker table. The Truman of the Hersey tale, which was finished just before the Key West writer's death in 1993, invents a new poker variation called Key West: "Seven card stud with deuces, sevens, and all four queens wild. And of course the jokers." When an aide suggests that this gives away too many freebies, Truman speaks a volume on the nature of the tropical island he had adopted: "You could say that.... A person could say Key West does that."

Just down the block at 205 Whitehead Street sits the **Audubon House**. Originally known as the John Geiger House, the two-story clapboard was renamed by the couple who restored the old schooner pilot's residence in 1960. John James Audubon, author of the *Ornithological Biography*, was most likely the very first writer to spend considerable time in Key West. He visited the island in 1832 to identify new species for his portfolio and to fill his journal. While in Key West, the naturalist painted several exquisite aviary portraits for his encyclopedic *Birds of America*. The diarist was so taken with the place that he wrote, "I have taken it upon myself to name this species [a brown pigeon dove] the Key West Quail or Key West Pigeon and offer it as a tribute to the generous inhabitants of the island who favored me with their friendship." Audubon's host for the visit was Benjamin Strobel, a newspaper editor who apparently located the gorgeous flame-colored tree used as a backdrop for a pair of white-crowned pigeons the ornithologist was painting. That same tree, commonly called a Geiger tree, still flowers in the gardens of the Whitehead Street house today.

Ask the knowledgeable museum-shop staff to point out the very precise painting of Key West which forms the background of the great white heron bookplate. For collectors, the shop has an excellent selection of well-priced first-edition plates from Audubon's London-engraved and hand-colored series.

Just a jaunt from Whitehead in the direction of the Atlantic, the unrestored blocks around Thomas Street at Petronia look much as they did in Hemingway's time. The **Blue Heaven Restaurant** (729 Thomas St.) has retained the rough-and-tumble atmosphere the building had when Old Hem, as he called himself, showed up for the Friday night fights. The professional matches were held in the side yard, scene of today's alfresco service at picnic tables.

It is not farfetched to imagine Hemingway sparring with his old pal Archibald MacLeish in Key West. Poet extraordinaire MacLeish had been a boxing partner to Hemingway in Europe before the many trips he made to the southernmost key to catch up with this longtime friend.

NOTE: For the less-than-hearty miler, it's good to remember that bicycle-powered pedicabs can be hailed right near the corner of Front and Duval Streets. Pedaled by able and fit exercise maniacs, they still offer a leisurely pace for getting an overview of the area and a feel for the designated sites. The cabs are an easy perch from which to plan a return assault on the most captivating locations.

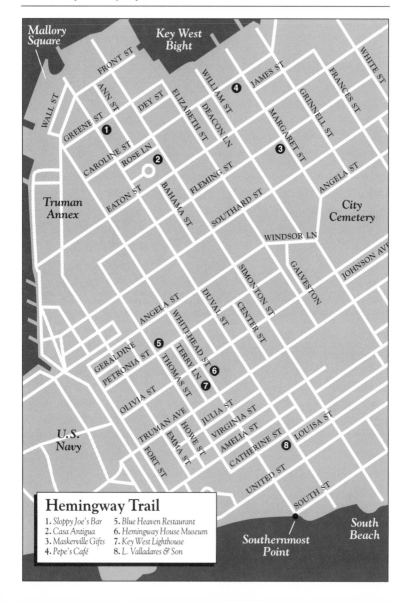

Hemingway Trail

Old friend John Dos Passos tipped him off to the tropical jewel at
the southern tip of Florida; the Peninsular & Occidental Steamship
Company brought him here on the Havana-Key West run; and his
wife Pauline's Uncle Gus Pfeiffer bankrolled the trip (plus a new
Ford and an island house, too). But once **ERNEST HEMINGWAY**
(1899–1961) got to Key West, he did all the rest himself—the
fishing, the carousing, the boxing, the gambling, the speakeasy-
hopping, and the writing.

Most of all there was the writing. Key West's literary life would
never be the same again; nor would Hemingway's. He wrote five
novels and some of his most brilliant short stories in the Key West
years. In the spectacular waters surrounding the island, he mastered
angling and the mythic sport of big-game fishing that would inform
his life, his legend, and his last novel, *The Old Man and the Sea*,
which garnered him the 1954 Nobel Prize.

Key West seems to foster excesses, and no one lived up to these
excesses better than Ernest Hemingway. For a glimpse into the
author's outsized way of life in Key West, begin at the corner of
Duval and Greene Streets at the saloon he made famous, **Sloppy
Joe's Bar** (200 Duval St.). Originally a shack across from the Navy
base, Sloppy Joe's moved to 428 Greene Street and went "legit" at
the end of Prohibition in 1933 before moving to its current location
on Duval Street in 1937.

Named for owner Joe Russell, a charterboat captain-turned-
publican and occasional rumrunner during the Prohibition years,
the speakeasy became headquarters for what Hemingway called his
"mob." The author formed an instantaneous friendship with Russell
when the barman cashed a royalty check from Scribner's (most
probably from *The Sun Also Rises*) for more than a thousand dollars

in the first weeks of Hemingway's island stay. A leading local bank had refused the same check in that spring of 1928.

Prohibition was a foreign concept to the swashbuckling sea town. In fact, a number of newspaper writers of the day suggested that "Hoover Gold" (the profits from bootlegging) was a genuine boon for the island economy. Hemingway had his pick of 40 or more speakeasy clubs and strip palaces when choosing a watering hole. However, he remained faithful to Joe Russell's even after the "Great Experiment" was repealed.

Hemingway's novel (and the popular 1944 movie version with Humphrey Bogart) *To Have and Have Not* was set in a Key West bar very much like Sloppy's. It was called Freddy's Bar in the book, and the character of Freddy Wallace is said to have been modeled after Joe Russell. Like Joe, barkeep Freddy also owned a charterboat, the aptly named *Queen Conch*. There is a delicious scene in the film when 19-year-old Lauren Bacall, making her screen debut, sings at Hoagy Carmichael's piano, evoking the same seedy tropical barroom feel that Sloppy Joe's has today. Except for the addition of glaringly amplified rock bands in the evening, Hemingway's favorite oasis has remained much as it was the last time he ordered there.

The raucous bar has also inadvertently served as a repository of literary gold. While divorcing wife Pauline to marry journalist Martha Gelhorn (whom he first met at Sloppy Joe's in 1936), Hemingway cleared pounds of original manuscripts, galley proofs, and personal papers out of their Key West house in 1940 and dumped them in the back room of Russell's bar. Russell died in 1941, and the new saloon owners never unlocked the room full of Hemingway's belongings, sure the author would claim them in one of his several return visits. He never did.

The treasures at Sloppy Joe's remained untouched until a year after Hemingway's death in 1961, when his fourth wife, Mary, rescued them. Some of the unearthed memorabilia hangs framed on the walls of the bar today, including two uncashed royalty checks from the 1930s. One story claims that pulled from the stash was the forgotten manuscript of *A Moveable Feast*, Hemingway's delightful memoir of Paris. Rich with his most personal descriptions of the City of Light, it was published posthumously in 1964. Other valuable records from the Sloppy Joe's find were given to local historian Betty Barnes, wife of Hemingway factotum Toby Barnes. Librarian Barnes organized them into the Hemingway Collection of the Monroe County Library, now housed in Key West's library at 700 Fleming Street.

One particularly precious literary and historical artifact remains a must-see at Sloppy Joe's Bar. The picture hanging on the bar's south wall is a prime example of the stylized neoclassical work done by the WPA artists during the Depression. Joe Russell commissioned the original from Erik Smith, one of several painters and writers sent to Key West in the early 1930s under the federal government's Artists and Writers Project. The picture, an exact copy of the original mural, forever glorifies the Hemingway mob's drinking days in Key West. The work, which depicts a Bacchus-like Hemingway donning a crown of grape leaves and surrounded by his usual bar mates, is itself worth a trip to Sloppy Joe's.

Just one block east and one more south of Sloppy Joe's is the Casa Antigua building (314 Simonton St.), the Hemingways' first address in Florida. En route from Paris to the United States via Havana in 1928, the young couple had not even planned an over-night stay in Key West. Upon their arrival, a brand-new Model A Ford, ordered as a gift by Pauline Hemingway's uncle, was to be waiting at the docks for the trip north. The car was delayed for several days, and a furious Hemingway was placated by the local Ford dealer, who offered him the company rooms in the apartment building over the Trevor and Morris auto showroom. Called Casa Antigua, the private residence today looks much as it did during

Hemingway's stay, minus the showroom windows. A shop called **Pelican Poop** (a moniker of which Hemingway would surely approve) is housed in one of the old Ford garages. Inquire there about the self-guided tour of the ultra-tropical gardens in what used to be the Hemingways' courtyard.

The vagaries of car delivery circa 1930 and serendipity itself forged a new history for Hemingway and, no doubt, for American literature, too. While working on *A Farewell to Arms* in the small suite of rooms, Hemingway wrote to friends around the country, extolling the virtues of his newfound playground in the sun. Hemingway beckoned writers John Dos Passos and Archibald MacLeish and painters Waldo Pierce and Henry Strater to join him. It seems likely that in one of these missives Hemingway first penned the sobriquet he used to describe Key West—"the St. Tropez of the poor"—a name that would endure for decades.

Hemingway arranged accommodations with a one-dollar-a-day tariff for his visiting friends at the Overseas Hotel (917 Fleming St., now a private house). In the morning, the writer took visitors to Mrs. Baker's Electric Kitchen (830 Fleming St.) for his daily breakfast of Cuban bread, a glass of milk, and a glass of Vichy water. The café was run by Mrs. Rhoda Baker, introduced as "Rutabaga" by Hemingway, who was given to nicknaming anyone he liked. The unique wooden awning that wraps around the structure still holds the ceramic separators installed when it was the first in the neighborhood to be electrified. Looking virtually as it did in the 1930s, the building now houses **Maskerville Gifts**, a stylish boutique for curios, sculpture, American crafts, and hand-fashioned feather goods including masks, headdresses, and even lampshades.

Two blocks down William Street toward the Gulf leads to Caroline Street and **Pepe's Café** (806 Caroline St.), whose sign declares it the "Eldest Eating House in the Florida Keys, Est. 1909." The original Pepe's was moved to Caroline Street in the late 1960s from lower Duval Street, where Hemingway would have known the café's Cuban food and ice cubes in the men's room urinals, a hygienic nicety picked up in the Paris of old and still practiced at Pepe's today.

Cutting diagonally across Old Town (about eight blocks in a southwest direction), one can discover the unreconstructed fishing-village funkiness Hemingway thrived on. **Blue Heaven Restaurant** (729 Thomas St.) is an open-air eatery on the site of an outdoor boxing ring where Hemingway refereed his beloved sport. Every Friday night found him at the center of matches between the island's considerable number of professional pugilists. The house adjacent to the one-time boxing area once held a dance hall and bordello. Today it holds the restaurant's small kitchen, along with an art studio. Island lore holds that Hemingway himself was a client of the second floor "cribs." Given the nature of the business conducted upstairs, records were not kept to document the author's presence. Hemingway only fraternized for certain at the ground-level games.

A few blocks south of Blue Heaven Restaurant at 907 Whitehead Street is the house the Hemingways bought in 1931 as their permanent address. It was a grand acquisition: a Spanish Colonial-style villa made of native stone on more than an acre of land (considered vast by the town's standards). Soon filled with antiques, art, and hunting trophies collected during eight years in Europe, the showplace became a salon for many of the Key West writers of the day.

Pauline Hemingway made a major addition to the garden when she put in a swimming pool to surprise her husband, an avid swimmer, upon his return from covering the civil war in Spain in 1937. The island's first, the pool had to be dug with pick and shovel into the brutally hard coral rock for the astronomical sum of $20,000 (more than $250,000 today). On hearing the price, Hemingway

Hemingway House

reportedly threw down a Lincoln copper and exploded, "Here, you might as well take my last cent." The penny is still embedded in the patio surrounding the pool today, right where Pauline had it put and covered with glass.

The famed penny, the Spanish tiles used for interior decoration and said to be laid by the author himself, and of course, the writing studio over the poolhouse are just a few of the draws to the **Hemingway House Museum**. Opened to the public in 1964 by the owners who bought it from Hemingway's estate, the house now daily attracts 600 to 800 devotees who revel in the quick-paced recitation on the novelist's Key West life and literary output.

Strictly disciplined to cross the catwalk over to his writing room every morning before eight, Hemingway produced in Key West some of his most famous works: *A Farewell to Arms*, *Death in the Afternoon*, *Green Hills of Africa*, *To Have and Have Not*, *For Whom the Bell Tolls*, and "The Snows of Kilimanjaro." He wrote his manuscripts in longhand in pencil, a fact he revealed in a celebrated interview in 1957 by George Plimpton for the *Paris Review*. Hemingway explained to Plimpton that a truly good day's work produced seven pencils' worth of prose.

A few doors up and across the way from Hemingway House is the **Key West Lighthouse** (938 Whitehead St.), which Hemingway would have seen from the wrought iron balcony outside his bedroom. Now maintained by the Key West Art and Historical Society, the pretty property has a small museum with exhibits celebrating the 200-year history of America's lighthouses.

Climb the 88 steps up the spiral staircase for a terrific overlook of Old Town and of the Navy waterfront. In the old submarine basin outlined by the cement barriers, Hemingway berthed his prized boat *Pilar*, bought with advance monies for some *Esquire* short stories in 1934.

The same Navy waters provided a swimming hole for Hemingway in the pre-pool years of 1928 through 1936. After writing all morning and before his daily stop at Sloppy Joe's around three o'clock, he would trek the few blocks to the Navy base, which was virtually abandoned between World War I and World War II. Through well-connected local friends, Hemingway got

Key West Lighthouse

the military go-ahead for everyday bathing privileges. Very often he would have the company of "Dos," as Hemingway dubbed John Dos Passos, a charter member of Papa's band whenever his fellow writer was in town.

The proprietor of **L. Valladares & Son**, the Fleming Street newsstand, delighted in this coterie. It was none other than the 28-year-old Ernest Hemingway who first suggested to Leonte Valladares that he would buy the New York and other big city newspapers if the local news vendor would only stock them. Luckily for current visitors to the island, the legacy of that exchange lives on today at L. Valladares & Son (now moved to 1200 Duval St.), where more than 150 out-of-town and foreign papers and magazines fill the racks each week. Still run by members of the same Cuban family as during Hemingway's day, the large store is a periodical paradise for serious news hounds. Full of poetry journals and literary reviews, it begs for an hour or two browse from vacationing print junkies.

Tennessee Walk

The journey outlined in the Tennessee Walk attempts to give a sense of Tennessee Williams' own eccentricity and contradictions. To follow the itinerary is to begin to understand the dramatist's enormous energy. What ordinary mortal could make the daily—and nightly—rounds described and also write 65 plays, almost 200 poems and short stories, screenplays, novellas, and a riveting autobiography? For the more than 40 years that **TENNESSEE WILLIAMS** (1911–1983) graced the shores of Key West, his opus was staggering.

When Thomas Lanier Williams (Tom, for short) made his initial visit to Key West in 1941, his life as a professional playwright was just beginning to come together. His alter-ego name—Tennessee Williams—had been first used only a few years before on a 1938 application form for the distinguished Group Theater Prize. The promising writer won the award and went on to secure an important New York agent and a contract for the prestigious Theater Guild to produce his play *Battle of Angels*, which debuted in 1941.

For some gossipy background reading to the Tennessee Walk, try *Memories of Key West* by Lee Dodez. Still a resident, Dodez was a visitor to the Williams house, and he knew most of the Tennessee circle: Henry Faulkner, the offbeat artist who lived with a goat named Alice and who gave Williams painting lessons; Frank Philip Merlo, the truest of Williams' loves; Stell Adams, Tennessee's cousin who always accompanied his mad sister Rose on Key West visits and finally stayed on to make a career of palm-reading; and Frank Fontis, the wiley friend who fashioned the author's much-loved gazebo.

An appropriate starting point for a waltz around Tennessee's Key West is the **Waterfront Playhouse** (400 block of Wall St.).

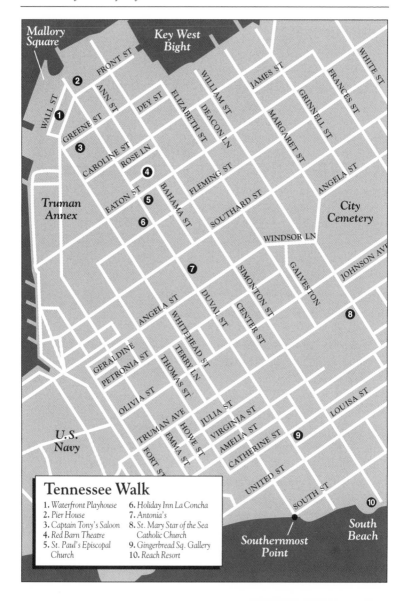

Tennessee Walk

1. *Waterfront Playhouse*
2. *Pier House*
3. *Captain Tony's Saloon*
4. *Red Barn Theatre*
5. *St. Paul's Episcopal Church*
6. *Holiday Inn La Concha*
7. *Antonia's*
8. *St. Mary Star of the Sea Catholic Church*
9. *Gingerbread Sq. Gallery*
10. *Reach Resort*

Home to the Key West Players, the Waterfront is where Williams read from his own works to a packed house in 1970. Dressed in a white summer suit, the soft-spoken playwright raised funds for a library expansion program in which he was involved. Such beautiful writings as "Prudence in Kings" and "Remember Me as One of Your Lovers" brought the audience to ovation time and again.

A prominent patron of local theater, Williams was a frequent ticket holder at the Waterfront Playhouse, which regularly staged productions of his plays in the 1960s and 1970s. Imagine the enthralled residents seeing *Cat on a Hot Tin Roof* or *The Glass Menagerie* only a few seats away from the author himself. Still more exciting for resident thespians was Williams' involvement in a 1976 staging of *Suddenly Last Summer* at the now defunct Greene Street Theater. In the back rows of the tiny hall, the playwright apparently reworked lines right on through the dress rehearsal and into the night, even considering a new ending for his 1958 stunner. More recently, the Waterfront produced a Williams classic that would have greatly moved the dramatist. His younger brother Dakin Williams in full faded, southern-belle drag did a turn as the immortal Blanche Dubois in a humorous rendition of the often-interpreted *A Streetcar Named Desire*, Williams' 1948 Pulitzer Prize winner. How Tennessee would have applauded!

For the next stop on the Tennessee tour, move east on Front Street and cross the bottom of Duval Street into the **Pier House** (One Duval St.), a regular stomping ground for Tennessee Williams when the resort was newly opened in 1965. He held court on the decks overlooking the diminutive beach, lounging the afternoon away with out-of-town literates such as Gore Vidal and Truman Capote. At the beach café or the more elegant waterfront dining room, agents and producers, celebrities and wannabes swirled in Williams' giant wake like minnows in a maelstrom.

The hotel was the venue in 1980 for Williams' 69th birthday

bash, hosted by Pier House owner David Wolkowsky. It was un-
equivocally the hottest ticket in town that night. The Pier House
continues those Williams' ties today by lending support to the
Founder's Society, the group that spearheads most of the fund-
raising for the Tennessee Williams Fine Arts Center. Williams
attended the 1980 dedication of the theater, which is located at Key
West's community college campus on neighboring Stock Island.

Today's Pier House is also home to an old Williams favorite:
headliner Bobby Nesbitt, who used to gentle the ivories for Tennessee at the Claire Restaurant (now **Bogart's** on upper Duval Street).
The charming Nesbitt continues to wow a standing-room-only
crowd five nights a week from his grand piano bar with a high-
society cabaret style.

The Pier House piano bar would indeed appeal to the writer
who was a world-class pub-crawler. After a long morning of writing
and an afternoon's loll at one of his preferred beaches, Tennessee
Williams embraced the night. The Duval Club (today **Captain
Tony's Saloon** at 428 Greene St.) held particular appeal for Williams who was said to favor its electric combination of hard-core
barflies and boys in uniform. The rough-hewn bar remained a Navy
saloon during the postwar boom years.

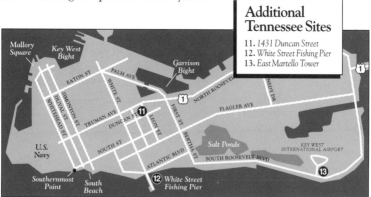

Additional Tennessee Sites

11. *1431 Duncan Street*
12. *White Street Fishing Pier*
13. *East Martello Tower*

The establishment kept Williams' attention even after its name change in 1958 to Captain Tony's when new owner Tony Tarracino rechristened it. A former mayor of Key West, Tarracino was often described by locals as a "dropout from a Hemingway novel."

Tennessee Williams' arrival in Key West coincided with the World War II buildup at the island's naval base. It was clearly a free-wheeling Navy town with all the rowdy nighttime distractions which that implies. Even in the postwar years of the 1940s and 1950s, there was more than enough seedy sundown action to go around. One Navy commander reported back to Washington, "Duval Street is a wide-open, honky-tonk area studded with bars and so-called 'night clubs' of fairly tawdry character." Apparently the Navy was often tempted to declare the entire town off-limits to enlisted personnel. Reason languished, however, and Navy men continued to drink happily with the locals.

Although the truly tawdry is just a memory, a certain unrepressed spirit still flourishes on the island. It remains secure in a city that has always nurtured the kind of tolerance Tennessee Williams valued so much. Certainly one of the most well-known personalities to openly espouse a gay lifestyle long before that was *au fait* in the United States, Tennessee Williams would be proud of the easy communication that exists among the clientele at Captain Tony's today: bikers and business owners; sensitive writers and womanizing seamen; spring breakers and octogenarians. Such is the blend that makes Key West the bohemian cocktail that so appeals to artists and writers. The names on the 60 or so barstools at Captain Tony's indicate some of the best bohemians in modern literature. Saunter in and sit atop the same seats once held by Gore Vidal, Truman Capote, Carson McCullers, Budd Shulberg, S. J. Perelman, Tennessee Williams, and many more.

The year before Williams visited Key West, he had split his time between New York and Provincetown, writing arduously but seemingly unable to produce a commercially successful play. A true southerner, Williams was desperate for respite from the wet, cold northeastern winters. When one of his friends mentioned her mother's hostelry in the warmth of Key West, he took the hint gladly.

The Tradewinds was a guesthouse on the corner of Caroline and Duval. It was owned by Mrs. Cora Black, the mother of Marion Vaccaro, Tennessee Williams' great friend to whom he dedicated his 1957 drama, *Orpheus Descending*. Built before the Civil War, the Tradewinds was originally known as the Caroline Lowe Mansion. Novelist David Loovis, who worked at the guesthouse during Tennessee's time there, offers a fictionalized account of the Tradewinds' high times in his 1961 *The Last of the Southern Winds*. Very sadly, in 1966, the Tradewinds was consumed by fire. The conflagration of dreams and memories left nothing in its place but an uninteresting concrete structure.

To imagine the feel of the Tradewinds in Tennessee Williams' day, one can turn to the Milton W. Curry Mansion (511 Caroline St.). A hotel today, the **Curry Mansion Inn** offers lodging that gives a look-see into the life of upper-crust Key West, circa 1905. That was when the house was built by the Curry family with an inheritance from the estate of William Curry, Florida's first millionaire and richest man when he died at the turn of the century.

By the time Mrs. Black turned the Caroline Lowe house into the Tradewinds, its own grandeur had given way to genteelness. In February 1941 Tennessee Williams checked into the bridal suite for his first winter night on the island. Fully enchanted by the charm of Key West, he finagled a long-term lease for the former slave quarters out back. Bath facilities were added to the outbuilding for his comfort during his first lengthy stay.

The transplanted writer began to work successfully in that little house. There he was able to shake off the gloom of the northern cold and of the disappointing reviews of the recent Boson test-run of his play *Battle of Angels*. He played successfully, too: the Tradewinds piano bar was the red-hot center of Key West's hotshot nightlife, and Williams was usually there.

A short block up Duval Street leads to the **Red Barn Theatre**, another stage known to Tennessee Williams. The gracious red-brick house at 319 Duval Street shields from view the intimate theater. Take a stroll up the driveway for a look at the tiny converted stable where the playwright watched two of his new one-act plays debut in the 1950s. One of these may have been the basis for the screenplay *Baby Doll* which was to bring controversy into Williams' life. When the movie premiered in 1956, Cardinal Francis Spellman himself denounced the film from the altar of New York's St. Patrick's Cathedral. *Time* magazine called *Baby Doll* "just possibly the dirtiest American-made motion picture that has ever been legally exhibited." Unsettling as all the brouhaha was, the reluctant celebrity contented himself with the afterglow of receiving the 1955 Pulitzer Prize for *Cat on a Hot Tin Roof*.

Farther along Duval stands **St. Paul's Episcopal Church** (401 Duval St.), which has often figured in the literary pages of Key West history. Benefit concerts on the massive 100-pipe organ have helped libraries and readers alike. Noted citizens of letters such as Philip Burton, distinguished Shakespeare scholar, playwright, poet, and adoptive father of the actor Richard, have given dramatic readings to aid church renovations. In 1954 the church served as one of the sets for the movie version of Williams' *The Rose Tattoo*. During filming, fans gathered at the church hoping to catch a moment with stars Burt Lancaster and Anna Magnani. Williams' poignantly drawn character Serafina gave the earthy Italian actress lines that would help win her the Best Actress Oscar for 1955.

Today St. Paul's, named for the apostle who also protects against shipwrecks, is a cultural centerpiece of the island's choral music community. It is the site of almost weekly concerts, often with outstanding chorales and string ensembles from around the country. Stop by the church to pick up a schedule.

Episcopal churches had often provided sanctuary for the young Tom Williams whose cherished maternal grandfather was an Anglican minister. Seeking refuge from an overbearing mother and the increasing madness of his mentally ill sister, the boy willingly lived in the various rectories where his grandfather was assigned.

The bond between Williams and his beloved relative was long-established by the time the playwright brought Grandfather Dakin to live in Key West at the **Hotel La Concha** (430 Duval St.). In January of 1947 Williams opted out of his Tradewinds accommodations and checked himself and the retired cleric into adjacent rooms at the top of the hotel. Built in 1925 for the new generations of driving tourists, the six-story lodge was Key West's skyscraper showcase. Twenty years later, the inn was still thriving and it provided Williams with just the right atmosphere for some serious daily work.

The object of Williams' La Concha toil was a play he called *The Poker Night*. The final version of the work about a brooding working-class stiff from New Orleans was later renamed *A Streetcar Named Desire*. It captured a Pulitzer Prize the next year, and Stanley, Stella, Blanche, and Mitch found their way into the permanent lexicon of the American theater. By May of 1948, when the award for *Streetcar* was announced, Williams had already determined that Key West greatly appealed to him. He always said he wrote best there; it was the place he was closest to being happy.

A bona fide restaurant rat, Tennessee Williams rarely dined at home. **Antonia's** (615 Duval St.), which opened in 1979, was a regular dinner stopover for Williams. The owners remember their famous customer as "sweet and shy." Good to the waiters and genuinely interested in the restaurant's progress, Williams preferred his usual table in the corner. He always ordered the Ruffino Ducale Chianti, the gold-labeled reserve bottle that was one of the choicest selections on Antonia's wine list at the time.

Antonia's certainly qualifies as a "white tablecloth restaurant," as Williams' grandfather would say. Grandfather Dakin, a frequent dinner partner of his favorite heir, was unstinting in his disdain for dining establishments that did not use cloth napkins. Williams immortalized this preference in *The Night of the Iguana* when Hannah makes a point to bring along proper napery for her grandfather. Antonia's—like **Logun's Lobster House** on the Atlantic end of Simonton (1420 Simonton St.) and the **Queen's Table** in the Santa Maria Motel (1401 Simonton St.) across from Logun's—is one of a handful of restaurants that remain basically as they were when Williams last summoned their sommeliers.

A few other favorite watering holes are right where the author left them; only the names have changed. His constant hangout during the 1970s was the Claire Restaurant (900 Duval St.). The wildly popular bistro and piano bar glowed through the nights of its ten-year run, with the playwright very much in evidence. Today, the veranda-fronted complex is home to Casablanca at Bogart's, where part of it is billed as an Irish Caribbean pub—the sort of bizarre tangle of identities that Tennessee Williams would inevitably have found delightfully twisted.

Down in the 200 block of Duval, the playwright would often usher in the late hours at Delmonico's (218 Duval St.), a restaurant and nightclub. Today at the old Delmonico's location stands **Rick's**, a saloon replete with twenty-somethings, loud music, and bar tabs full of beer. Its past, however, was full of rakish glamour. Hemingway wined and dined there in the 1930s whenever New York and Paris literati descended upon the town. Williams never met Hemingway during the Key West years, but he did form a friendship with Papa's ex, Pauline, who also frequented Delmonico's. She is pictured in the photo section of Williams' 1975 autobiography, and they saw each other often in their adopted hometown.

Local entertainer John "Ma" Evans fondly remembers a pre-dawn encounter with Williams at Delmonico's. When Evans requested an autograph from the retiring celebrity, he received a big smile and an "Of course, darling." "Forever Yours," the writer scribbled and demurely asked, "Now, can I have five dollars?" With the evening on the wane and his ready cash spent, the thirsty night owl was in need of another drink. Evans gladly complied, and the bartered autograph still hangs center stage on the cabaret star's apartment wall.

A far more serene spot on the Tennessee Walk sits at the corner of Truman Avenue and Winsdor Lane. The double-spired grandeur of **St. Mary Star of the Sea Catholic Church** (1010 Windsor Ln.) is reached by trekking up Duval and north a few blocks on Truman. In 1969 at the ornate baptismal font just inside the vestibule, a somewhat surprising candidate for conversion was taken into the Roman Catholic faith—the irreverent Tennessee Williams. Previously disinclined to practice any particular religion, the playwright drifted into Catholicism sometime after the death of his great love Frank Merlo.

The New Jersey-born Merlo had moved in with the author around 1950. A Catholic himself, Merlo most likely spent some time in the inviting St. Mary's, whose 12-foot louvers along all sides are open to welcome every passerby. The personal turmoil of Williams' life after the loss of his companion may explain his sudden outreach to organized religion, but readers of his plays know that Williams was always fascinated with mankind's relationship to God. Religious symbols and subtext lace several of his plays, perhaps none more overtly than *The Night of the Iguana*. A defrocked priest is a central player, and the search for soul and salvation echoes throughout the dialogue.

Back on Duval Street at Number 1207 is the **Gingerbread Square Gallery**, the longest-running art gallery in town. Begun in the early 1970s (then at 905 Duval St.), the Gingerbread showed the work of several local artists, such as John Kiraly, Sal Salinero, and Carol Sadowski, who would go on to carve out national reputations. Williams, who took up painting to relax, showed there as well and said that his second means of expression did not exhaust him the way writing did.

His paintings, many of which he gave to friends, were slow to sell at prices of $50 to $100 until after the writer's death. By the end of the 1980s, however, the brightly colored, broad-stroked oils with T.W. inscribed in the corner were rumored to fetch five figures. A year or two after Williams died, one of the original Gingerbread owners mounted a show of the writer's artwork borrowed from a few dozen locals fortunate enough to have the prized rarities. When asked about the exhibit, one devilish art patron exclaimed, "He was an excellent writer."

Ever lyrical, Tennessee Williams christened his pictures with wonderfully fanciful titles: *Fairy in a Wicker Chair*, *Recognition of Madness*, *Abandoned Chair Occupied Briefly*, *The Wine That Is Spilled*. Daubs though the paintings might be, their titles reflect the extraordinary mind of a wounded genius.

By the last half of the 1940s, Williams could feel artistically and financially secure. *The Glass Menagerie* had been an unqualified hit in New York. *Streetcar* was even bigger and won the Pulitzer, too. Moreover, his love for Key West was no infatuation; it was time to buy a house.

In 1950 he chose a small Caribbean-style cottage which he relocated from the waterfront of downtown to **1431 Duncan Street**, a less-populated area near the mangrove swamps. In the quiet neighborhood, Williams gradually embellished the property by adding a writing house, a guesthouse, a whimsical gazebo, and a big swimming pool inlaid with a great blooming rose tattoo design. In the solitude of the writing studio that stood beyond the pool, which he referred to as The Mad House, Williams churned out an unbelievable number of major works.

Tennessee William's "Summer House"

The level of achievement Williams attained in his uncluttered writing room was astonishing. With no outside doorknob and only one key—his own— the little house was his private world where no one was allowed to intrude. In complete privacy, the man who purportedly kept a photograph of Eugene O'Neill on his desk became in Key West O'Neill's equal: the other greatest American playwright.

The Williams enclave was certainly not for work only. The playwright entertained an illustrious gaggle of guests in his front garden in the gazebo, named the "Jane Bowles Summer House" for his friend the playwright. Jane Bowles authored *In the Summer House* about which Williams wrote "[it] stands quite superbly alone among works for the American theater." The gazebo was the scene of more than one infamous cocktail hour. Glass in hand, bons mots at the ready, stars studded the summer house, including Carson McCullers, Françoise Sagan, Truman Capote, Talullah Bankhead, Gore Vidal, and Christopher Isherwood.

The bright red-shuttered Duncan Street house which for so many years was alive and full of energy with the Williams crowd sadly sat empty and lonesome for almost ten years before it was sold in 1992 to resident owners.

As it had been for Ernest Hemingway, a daily dip was a necessity for Tennessee Williams. He and his grandfather, he and his guests, he and his fellow writers would gather at one of the three beaches he designated superior swimming holes. **South Beach**, the pocket strand with the Caribbean feel, is at the Atlantic end of the island between Simonton and Duval. Gussied up a bit since the playwright's plunges, which were often au naturel, South Beach today is home to a tasteful little inn set back in the palms and a terrace-fronted restaurant near the water's edge.

The only natural sand beach on the island, the **Reach Resort**, lies nearby at the end of Simonton Street. Before the big pink hotel replaced it, the beach bungalow was known as the Sands Beach Club. It was a prime watering hole, literally and figuratively, for Williams and many of the town's other published sunbathers.

About a seven-block meander through the Casa Marina residential neighborhood that sprawls between Duval Street and Atlantic Boulevard brings the touring beach lover to the long **White Street Fishing Pier** (White St. at the Atlantic Ocean).

South Beach

During the 1970s, novelist and screenwriter James Leo Herlihy would meet Williams for a swim there most days. The young writer of *Midnight Cowboy* and *Blue Denim* had been a Tennessee Williams worshipper long before they met in Key West. Nearby **Higgs Beach** and the old **West Martello Tower** (Atlantic Blvd. near Reynolds St.), which houses botanical displays for the Key West Garden Club, are bonuses of a walk to the water.

Wander about a mile farther up the Atlantic beaches to find a Civil War citadel which doubles as the headquarters of the Art and Historical Society (3501 So. Roosevelt Blvd.). Called the **East Martello Tower**, the small but well-conceived museum contains the Key West Authors' Exhibit and an art gallery featuring native sculptor Mario Sanchez, whose work Tennessee Williams collected. For 60 years the octogenarian has produced winsome wood-carvings like the ones he does now at his alfresco

Key West Custom House

"studio" in the old cigar-makers village on Catherine Street. Born in Key West, the Cuban artist carves under the trees in the back of his brother's cottage. The full-color bas-reliefs of familiar Key West street scenes capture the spirit of the island and preserve its history in an ongoing tableau.

The collection of the East Martello holds such genuine gems as a story handwritten by the 11-year-old Ernest Hemingway and a number of Tennessee Williams' scripts with their characteristic heavy blue-penciled edits. These finds are rotated into the standing exhibition along with mementos from scores of nationally acclaimed writers. More room for the permanent display of literary memorabilia is expected when the museum moves by the end of the decade to the recently renovated Key West Custom House at the Gulf end of Whitehead Street.

The East Martello is also where one can learn about Key West's glittering prize winners. The tiny island has more pounds per square foot of Nobel and Pulitzer Prize writers than any other literary city. Nobel laureate Ernest Hemingway won for *The Old Man and the Sea* in 1954. Repeat Pulitzer honorees have been Robert Frost (in 1924, 1931, 1937, and 1943) and Tennessee Williams (in 1948 and 1955). Rounding out the Pulitzer awardees are: John Hersey (1945); Wallace Stevens (1955); Elizabeth Bishop (1956); Richard Wilbur (1957); Philip Caputo (1972); Joseph P. Lash (1972); James Kirkwood (1976); James Merrill (1977); and Alison Lurie (1985). The photomontage of award winners that hangs in the Martello is the work of Key West's Rollie McKenna, a first-class photojournalist who stands alone as a recorder of literary notables. A galaxy of stellar scribes is captured in her book, *A Life in Photography*.

NOTE: For a very personal take on Tennessee Williams' last few years, look into Lynn Mitsuko Kaufelt's sensational *Key West Writers and Their Houses*.

Detours: Other Writers and Their Digs

The spectre of Key West's two most writerly ghosts looms large. Hemingway's macho, burly, deep-sea spirit; Tennessee's sour-sweet fallen angel. But these were only a couple of the scores of scribes who were drawn to the outré quality of the island existence. In Key West writers could be rebellious expatriates without ever leaving the United States. So the writers came, years before Hemingway.

During the Civil War, correspondents came here to report Union news from the always contrary island—the southernmost city to declare for the North. Later, José Martí, the revolutionary magazine editor and political refugee, arrived to continue coverage on Cuba's War of Independence. With the Spanish-American War raging in neighboring Cuba in 1898, the island, then Florida's largest city, was catapulted into national newspaper headlines. In response to the war, the Hearst papers sent Frederic Remington and Richard Harding, hard-copy household names of the era, to file from Key West.

A continuing stream of writers, poets, and playwrights showed up after the conflicts ended. Jack London, Stephen Crane, Wallace Stevens, Robert Frost, Thornton Wilder, Upton Sinclair, and Zane Grey were seduced by the unspoiled beauty of the island. So even if fate had taken Hemingway and Williams elsewhere, Key West would still have word power to spare.

The listing of littérateurs and their related landmarks that follows is presented to give the reader a touchstone. One can get a feel for the astounding accumulation of talent on the island just by glancing through the list of authors. The devoted stroller can go one step further. Plug these additional landmarks into the previous walks for even richer detours into creative territory.

1401 Pine Street. This double-porched Conch house was rented in 1934 by **JOHN DOS PASSOS** (1896–1970) and his new wife Katy, whom he met at the Hemingways' house. Dos Passos had originally pointed Ernest Hemingway to Key West in the 1920s. Hemingway had endured almost a decade of the dank and drear of Parisian winters, when Dos Passos wrote him a letter that it was time for "Ole Hem" to go west and south "to dry out his old bones."

Kinetic by nature, Dos Passos traveled vastly, circling the world, crisscrossing the nation, listening to the people—soaking up what America had to say as it twisted from its agricultural past into its industrial future. Dos Passos would then bring it all back to Key West where he worked on *In All Countries* and *Three Plays*. He also worked on the trilogy that would become the epic *USA*. Dos Passos wrote to the critic Edmund Wilson that Key West was "a swell little jumping off place—the one spot in America desperately unprosperous," and that "life there was agreeable calm and gently colored with Bacardi."

Casa Marina Resort, 1500 Reynolds Street. The Flagler-built grand hotel was winter home to poet **WALLACE STEVENS** (1879–1955) from 1922 until the government took it over to billet troops during World War II. In his ode, "The Idea of Order at Key West," Stevens wrote that the island "sang beyond the genius of the sea ... a summer sound repeated in a summer without end." This poem was a particular favorite of Tennessee Williams, who requested that it be read at his funeral. Perhaps the summer without end is what the playwright sought from eternity.

It was at the Casa Marina that Stevens began a friendship with fellow New Englander **ROBERT FROST** (1874–1963). Frost spent a few seasons at the beachfront resort before moving to what is now known as the Robert Frost Cottage at the Heritage House Museum. In a 1940 interview in the *Key West Citizen*, Frost explained, "A poem begins with a lump in the throat, a homesickness or a love

Robert Frost Cottage

sickness." Home-sick is exactly how the poet sounded in an early letter from Key West. He fretted about the torpid weather and the cultural poverty. But he did allow one bright note in the critical missive. "People who know," he wrote, "say it is a Honolulu five thousand miles nearer home." All the skepticism in Frost's New England mind must have soon been overcome by the island's magical properties. He was to visit Key West for three more decades.

624 White Street. **ELIZABETH BISHOP** (1911–1979), whose "indisputed eminence" and "perfectionist poems" were discussed in a 1994 *Washington Post* review of her book *One Art: Letters*, lived in this 19th-century house for ten years before moving away in the mid-1940s. She earned a Pulitzer Prize in 1956 for *Poems: North & South: A Cold Spring*. When the Bishop residence was designated a literary landmark, Bishop's friend and preeminent poet James Merrill pronounced the dedication.

A winter resident of Key West, **JAMES MERRILL** (1926–1995) was called "the obvious heir to W. H. Auden" in the *New York Times Book Review*. One critic for *Solares Hill*, the weekly newspaper that best covers Key West's intellectual life, attributes Merrill's success to the fact that he "put the act of writing poetry at the center of his life … the arena where he lived most intensely." So successful was he that Merrill captured a 1976 Pulitzer Prize, two National Book Awards, and the prestigious Bollingen, among many other honors the literary world can bestow. Before his death in 1995, James Merrill spent more that a dozen seasons at **702 Elizabeth Street**.

Another Bishop friend and visitor to the house on White Street is **JOHN MALCOLM BRINNIN** (1916–), a poet in his own right and one of the United States' foremost experts on that genius of modern poetry, Dylan Thomas. An elegant biographer and historian, Brinnin maintained a correspondence with Bishop throughout her lifetime. He also successfully weathered the stormier seas inherent in a friendship with Truman Capote. His memoir *Truman Capote: Dear Heart, Old Buddy* is both charming and revealing. A gentleman scholar and former director of the Poetry Center in New York, Brinnin first vacationed in Key West in the 1940s and returned in the 1970s to take up permanent residence. He is considered the unofficial dean of the island's current corps of writers.

701 and 703 Fleming Street. The twin houses so noticeably good-looking across the street from Key West's pink library are the legacy of Broadway sparkler **JERRY HERMAN** (1933–). The composer, writer, and perennial Tony Award winner was instrumental in the gentrification of residential Old Town in the 1970s. Herman led many of his colleagues from the Hamptons smart set— leaders in publishing, design, and theater—to the now beautiful blocks around Elizabeth, Eaton, William, and Southard.

The proud pair on Fleming are just a couple of the houses to which Herman applied his polished theatrical touch. Best known for his score to *Hello, Dolly!*, Jerry Herman must have noted the fact that Thornton Wilder allegedly visited Key West during the time he worked on *The Matchmaker*. The Wilder play, of course, was the source for Herman's musical blockbuster.

Herman's fellow New Yorker **TRUMAN CAPOTE** (1924–1984) took readily to Key West but remained ever the houseguest. Perhaps this is not so surprising for the creator of Holly Golightly, the quintessential free spirit and heroine of *Breakfast at Tiffany's*. Apparently the diminutive dynamo tried to take up residence. According to real estate gossip, the day Capote was to settle on his new house, it was burgled. The property was then summarily rejected by the spooked author, who forever gave up the idea of Key West ownership. Befitting the consummate social butterfly, the writer visited often for the better part of three decades, and Capote tales abound—no doubt a source of pleasure to the devilish fanner of his own legendary flame.

The all-time showstopper has to be the famous Capote-meets-autograph-hound saga. Rumor holds that while at a local boîte with Tennessee Williams, Capote was beseeched by a bold young woman to autograph her navel. Always unflappable, he obliged. Presently an irate escort materialized, unzipped, and challenged the celebrity to "John Hancock" his private part. Without missing a beat, the wicked Capote quipped, "I don't know about an autograph, but perhaps I could initial it."

Typical writers' compound

New Moon Saloon, 1202 Simonton Street. Although the New Moon Saloon seems as if it were flash-frozen in 1967 and shipped in from the low-rent end of the Las Vegas strip, the place has curious appeal, decent food, and a definite soul. Open 24 hours a day, with happy hour from 1:00 a.m. to 4:00 a.m., the Moon is just the sort of roadhouse that might be frequented by the P.I. heroes of Key West's growing crop of crime-genre novelists. James W. Hall, David Kaufelt, John Leslie, Laurence Shames, and Stuart Woods are all enjoying justified success with their recent work in the fields of Raymond Chandler, Dashiel Hammett, and Florida's own John D. MacDonald.

Take, for example, Laurence Shames with his sequel to the highly praised *Florida Straits*. His motley Mafiosos turn up again in *Sunburn*, which was called "flashier than a Key West sunset" by the *New York Times Book Review*. Or try Gideon Lowry, the Conch hero of John Leslie's newest mystery *Night and Day*, which unravels its plot during Key West's annual Hemingway Days Festival. The

setting is a clever device used to poke fun at the cult-followers of Tennessee Williams and Ernest Hemingway, as well as at Key West literary types themselves.

The savvy, skillful, and stylish writing of David A. Kaufelt currently takes up life through Wyn Lewis, the heroine of his 1993 *The Fat Boy Murders* and his 1994 *The Winter Women Murders*. Both books are set in Waggs Neck Harbor, the town some reviewers suggest is fast becoming the new St. Mary Meade, Agatha Christie's fictional village that was home base to Miss Jane Marple. The plot revolves around the town's Annual Literary Symposium, a sly conceit for Kaufelt, who has provided some of the real lifeblood behind the real life Key West Literary Seminar.

Other local writers to turn to are Stuart Woods and James W. Hall. Hall's latest *Gone Wild* and his 1991 *Bones of Coral*, soon to be on film, are full of his usual gutsy portraits and crisp dialogue. With several published volumes of poetry to his credit, Hall has evocative descriptive powers rarely found in thrillers. Bestseller Woods also has numerous tense page-turners, including *Santa Fe Rules*, *L.A. Times*, *New York Dead*, and *Heat* in his repertoire of catchy titles.

Conch Grove (corner of Catherine and Watson Streets) and **Windsor Village** (Windsor Lane near Number 718). In the early 1970s, a number of ramshackle Conch cottages were converted into lushly planted clusters of attractive houses grouped around new communal pools. Writers, practitioners of one of the most solitary professions, seemed drawn to the compound model.

One of the first compounds, Conch Grove is located on the former site of 11 dilapidated cigar-makers' dwellings. It was more than half populated by novelists, journalists, and assorted refugees from New York publishing. The compound claimed as residents Pulitzer Prize-winning coauthor of *A Chorus Line* and *P.S. Your Cat Is Dead*, James Kirkwood; novelist David A. Kaufelt; publisher Ross Claiborne; *New York Times* writer Albin Krebs; and the popular literary agent Jay Garon.

On Windsor Lane, the compound housed neighbors John Hersey, Richard Wilbur, and John Ciardi, impressive for their sheer number of literary prizes, considerable scholarly output, and significant editorial impact upon American letters. Among Hersey's myriad works of fiction and nonfiction are the acknowledged classics

A Bell for Adano and *Hiroshima*. His *Key West Tales* was completed just before his death in 1993. *Molière Comedies* is former Poet Laureate and Pulitzer Prize winner Richard Wilbur's most recent adaptation for the Broadway stage. John Ciardi, before he died in 1986, lived at the compound after a remarkable career as poetry editor of the *National Review* and National Public Radio regular.

Mallory Square at sunset. A handful of 1960s and 1970s writers were among the original celebrants of the island's daily sunset ritual. Playwright James Leo Herlihy (*Midnight Cowboy*, *Blue Denim*, *The Season of the Witch*) was an acolyte of Tennessee Williams who befriended the young author and took a mentor's interest in his work. True to his talents as a screenwriter, Herlihy said that Key West in the old antiestablishment days was "a low-budget film noir mood piece." Tom McGuane's highly successful novels *The Bushwacked Piano* and *Ninety-Two in the Shade* depict some of the zanier inmates of that crazy era in Key West. Free love and good drugs, flower power and peace were the mantras that took McGuane and his friends into the enlightened new age. Not surprisingly, songwriter Jimmy Buffett, gonzo journalist Hunter Thompson, and heroic writer Jim Harrison were among this Key West contingent. The sunset countdown today still finds a number of leftover hippies at its fringe, wondering where the hundreds of photo-snapping tourists and street performers have come from and where the Age of Aquarius has gone to.

The hour or two before the sun's final flash is actually rather good fun—that genuine Key West hybrid of tacky and terrific. Hoop-jumping cats and their trainer hold their own version of the Cirque de Paris. The stark, still human statue completely covered in white pancake makeup and effecting marble is convincing enough to elicit a doubletake when he blinks. The cookie lady, the rubber-limbed contortionist shackled in chains, and the regulation snake charmer make it all seem like an old-fashioned buskers' ball.

621 Caroline Street. This beautifully symmetric house with gingerbread-worked porches on two levels was bought by **PHILIP CAPUTO** (1941–) just after his 1977 *A Rumor of War* hit the bestseller list. The Pulitzer Prize-winning journalist was Key West's first choice as Hemingway heir apparent. Both were foreign correspondents, both covered wars, and Caputo even fished for big game. In fact he hung his 500-plus-pound, record-setting sailfish in his favorite island pub. Sounds familiar. The novels Caputo proceeded to write from Key West were often top performers, among them *Horn of Africa* (1980), *DelCorso's Gallery* (1983), and *Indian Country* (1987).

1313 Reynolds Street. Novelist **ALISON LURIE** (1926–) spends time in New York, London, and this house in the Casa Marina neighborhood. Sometimes called America's Jane Austen, the writer and professor of American literature at Cornell University has long been visible at Key West literary functions. Author of *The War between the Tates* and *Imaginary Friends* among other serious hits, Lurie won the Pulitzer in 1985 for *Foreign Affairs*.

Simonton and Catherine Streets. This neighborhood used to be called Gato's Village in the late 1800s, when it was full of cigar-making Cubans who worked for factory owners such as E. H. Gato. A dozen huge cigar plants fueled the Key West economy and offered the working immigrants a particularly literary approach to on-the-job training. *Lectores*, as they were called, were the most cultured and scholarly members of the Cuban community who sat among the cigar-makers' benches and read poetry, plays, novels, and news of the day. The eager-to-learn workers paid the lectores' wages from their own pockets. More than one of the old and wise among today's Key West Cuban citizenry credit the cigar factory "professors" with enhancing their success.

Key West Cemetery. When Lawrence Ferlinghetti, the lead poet of the Beat Generation, came to participate in the 1994 Robert Frost Birthday Celebration, he headed for the cemetery at Margaret

Street and Passover Lane. He left with a new poem that finished, "I hear a faint crying from a hundred years ago." Plenty of history is embedded in the shallow burial ground atop the coral rock where most tombs are above ground. The always impeccable poet James Merrill referred to the sepulchers as "whitewashed hope chests." Typical of a town partial to both words and eccentrics, the Key West graveyard provides a good read. Look for the often-cited epitaph of the 50-year-old B. P. Roberts, "I told you I was sick," and for the grave of one Thomas Romer who was heralded as "Good citizen for 65 years. Lived to be 108. Unaccountable for 43 years."

The cemetery is the focus of a true account so grisly and macabre that only someone with the black humor of local writer Ben Harrison could have entitled his book about it *Undying Love*. The 1930's story of necrophilia and pathological perversion involves a grave-robbing X-ray technician obsessed with a beautiful young victim of tuberculosis. The monstrously mad scientist spent a seven-year "honey-

Sea oats

moon" with the wax-augmented body he dressed as his bride before he was found out. This shocking saga makes the simple oddity of burying the household pets—three dogs and a deer—in the rather grand Otto family plot seem rather mundane in comparison.

In *The Truth about Lorin Jones*, Alison Lurie writes of the Key West graveyard: "Soapy white marble and rough grey stone packing cases lay scattered in the long faded grass, like the debris of a freight-train wreck."

In contrast to the cemetery and decidedly less somber is the very lively Key West domicile of Jimmy Buffett, beyond the end of Riviera Drive alongside a canal. "Beware of Occupant" reads the inscription near the entrance gate. Just another little amusement courtesy of the Margarita Man.

Equally informative, albeit generally less humorous, are a number of other signs found around town on the walls and fences in various residential neighborhoods. These bronzed plaques signify literary landmarks designated by the Friends of Libraries USA, a national historical association that has chosen dozens of Key West sites for their select signage. Each marker honors a different author with a quote from his or her own writings. Look for them and discover even more detours along Key West's literary pathways.

Literary and Live

Perhaps it's the easygoing, community-oriented nature of the town. Maybe it's the decades-long commitment to the written word that started when the WPA Writers Project was sent to the island in the 1930s. Whatever the reason, dozens of literary events on the annual Key West calendar make for an incredibly vibrant resource that even short-term trippers can tap into with ease.

To catch up with the local literati, start on Fleming Street, where two of the very best sources of literary happenings are just a few blocks apart. **Key West Island Books** (513 Fleming St.) has the same mission as legendary bookstores Sylvia Beach's Shakespeare and Company in Paris or San Francisco's City Lights. More than just the low-key bookseller's shop it appears to be, Island Books conveys all that is book-wise in Key West.

Just inside the door is a wall full of books by the most recognized authors identified with Key West. Most are contemporary, and the quantity as well as the quality of the work is awe-inspiring. The staff is totally tuned to the reading rhythm of the island since they know so many of the writers who claim Key West as their permanent or winter habitat. The quiet browser is left to soak in the subtle atmosphere, while the more inquisitive bookworm is treated to considerable expertise, a bit of local booklore, and an update on coming events. These include the almost weekly book signings that are more like congenial wine tastings at which even first-time customers are invited to rub elbows with spotlighted scribblers.

A Hemingway hound, proprietor John Boisonault came to Key West for a three-week vacation in 1986. He wanted to experience firsthand the ambience of his hero and simply never left. A few months later the personable Boisonault bought the Fleming Street store. In addition to more conventional offerings, he has assembled a small but significant rare-book room with signed first editions and other remarkable tomes. Just lately, a first edition of *A Farewell to Arms* in the original dust jacket materialized. Signed by Hemingway and inscribed "Paris 1929," the year of publication, it was a literary groupie's concept of nirvana.

Farther along on Fleming Street, the pale pink one-story stucco building at Number 700 is a small-town library with a gargantuan soul exuding the spirit of a community in love with books. When the **Monroe County Key West Library** needed a lecture facility a few decades back, the town rallied to build an auditorium and named it for Tennessee Williams. Last year, a gloriously planted, bench-filled reading garden was funded by contributions from citizens like Poet Laureate Richard Wilbur, Pulitzer winners Alison Lurie and John Hersey, *Babar* author Jean de Brunhoff, and novelist David Kaufelt, among others.

The library's Florida History Room (which includes a biofile on all pertinent authors) is a haven for researchers and writers. Historian Tom Hambright presides. The genial curator is truly dedicated to his field and accessible to the generally curious as well as the professionally inclined. Setting the library apart from others of its size is a large collection of material kept in the vault which includes gems such as an original Hemingway journal. The library also holds first-Saturday-of-the-month book sales that provide a chance to cadge a find from famous local writers' discard shelves. The weekly lectures sponsored by the very active Friends of the Library group have hosted speakers as diverse as the poet Philip Burton, the bestselling crime novelist Laurence Shames, and pollster Louis Harris.

The library is a supporter of the nationally recognized **Key West Literary Seminar**. This nonprofit organization's stated purpose is to provide and preserve the island's literary heritage. Each January the seminar sponsors a conference that brings to the island literary figures from around the country to investigate a contemporary topic. In recent years, the seminars have explored biography, journalism, and screen writing, drawing such panelists as Pulitzer Prize winners David McCullough, James Merrill, David Halberstam, and Anna Quindlen. Held at the San Carlos Institute (516 Duval St.), the seminar's lectures, panels, and readings offer an expert's view of the topic at hand, with plenty of opportunity for the attendees to interact with the visiting writers and lecturers.

Under the auspices of the Key West Literary Seminar is a twice-weekly event that no self-avowed bibliophile should miss. Known as the **Writers' Walk**, the one-hour, one-mile tour covers some of the major sites in the literary life of the island that is currently full or part-time home to more than 80 published authors. Usually conducted by a local writer, the informative stroll provides a very personal look at Key West's writing life, past and present. One frequent guide is novelist David Kaufelt, a primary mover behind the Key West Literary Seminar activities. Meet at 10:30 a.m. Saturdays on the front porch of the Heritage House Museum (410 Caroline St.) or 10:30 a.m. Sundays in front of the Hemingway House (907 Whitehead St.). Tickets are sold at the meeting points or in advance at: Heritage House Museum (410 Caroline St.); Blue Heron Books (538 Truman Ave.); Caroline Street Books (800 Caroline St.); and Key West Island Bookstore (513 Fleming St.). NOTE: Tours are given from December through May; at other times a guided walk can be arranged by calling (305) 293-9291.

For drama buffs, the **Key West Theater Festival Office** is the place to be on Wednesday nights. A weekly play-reading group under sponsorship of the Waterfront Playhouse and the Key West Players is open to the public. Copies of the play of the week are distributed in advance, and a discussion of the work, the playwright, or the staging is led by one of the talents in Key West's theater world. Call the office at Duval Square (the plaza between Simonton and

Duval Streets), (305) 292-3725, to secure a copy of the play and any other needed information.

Poetry-in-motion is a good description for the several local events that take poetry off the page and onto the stage. Called "performance poetry" and "poetry slams," these spoken word fests are finding an enthusiastic audience for poetry presented as theater.

The **Red Barn Theatre** (319 Duval St.) has initiated a series for performing poets. Each one-night production joins the best in native talent with an out-of-town performer, many of whom are successful members on the national touring poet circuit. The six-event series runs from January through May, always on a Monday. To check on performance dates, call the theater at (305) 296-9911, or consult the Friday section of the *Key West Citizen* called "Paradise This Week." In fact, this daily paper is a fine source of information on all the performing arts for vacationing culture vultures.

Among the local newspapers, there is one absolute must-read. *Solares Hill* is the excellent weekly begun in the 1970s, the golden age of the free paper. The newspaper's editorial commitment to report upon the intellectual life of Key West has remained un-changed. Within its pages, the arts enthusiast will typically find one contemporary writer interviewing another in a relaxed setting without the influence of publicists or big-city editorial agendas. Recent issues have included pieces on or by the likes of Jane O'Reilly, Richard Wilbur, Joy Williams, Ellis Amburn, Alison Lurie, Barbara Ehrenreich, John Hersey, and Lawrence Ferlinghetti.

The **Appelrouth Grille** (Appelrouth Lane) might well be designated the unofficial checkpoint for true devotees of perfor-mance poetry. Owners Skip and Kat MacLeod sponsor the Appelrouth Literary Series which presents supercharged evenings full of open-mike readings, musical poems, spoken word artists, and more. In addition to the word-jams, the grill schedules at least weekly performances by one of the better-known fixtures on the local poetry and storytelling circuit, clever musical talent and author Ben Harrison. Call (305) 294-5662 for the lowdown on upcoming bookings.

Local poets Danne Hughes, Tony Klein, and Harry Calhoun have been tireless in keeping poetry on Key West's collective mind by originating slams. Before Appelrouth opened a few years ago, the trio built audiences at **Blue Heaven Restaurant** (729 Thomas St.) and the well-known **Green Parrot Bar** (601 Whitehead St.). Poetry happenings still happen at both. At the **Waterfront Playhouse** (Mallory Square) newcomers are welcome to test their verses every Thursday night from 6:00 to 8:00 p.m. before reaching for the spotlight on the more public stages.

Poetry readings with constructive feedback are the specialty of **Heritage House Museum** (410 Caroline St.). Budding poets in need of inspiration might find these groups appealing—none other than Robert Frost spent time around the old colonial house contemplating his own work. A core of nationally recognized Key West poets often lend their talents to Heritage House, including Dan Gerber, Judith Kazantzis, Marie Claire Blais, Phyllis Janowitz, Honor Moore, Kirby Congdon, and George Murphy. For the latest schedule of readings, call the very competent director Judith Gaddis at (305) 296-3573.

The poet pull to Key West has long been strong. There have been at least five poets honored by the Library of Congress as Poet Laureates who have taken up long refuge or residency on the island: Archibald MacLeish (1946); Elizabeth Bishop (1949); Robert Frost (1958); William Meredith (1978); and Richard Wilbur (1986).

Aspiring poets and fiction writers can also plan their visits around the Key West Literary Seminar's yearly week-long **Writers' Workshops**. Juried on their presubmitted writing samples, the attendees spend five mornings in lectures and discussion groups. Afternoons are reserved for individual consultations and critique

sessions with workshop leaders. Participants are then treated to a
weekend full of literary events such as beach and sunset readings,
book signings, a writer-oriented walking tour, and a reception with
local authors.

The usual agenda schedules the Fiction Workshop in February;
the Poetry Workshop in March to coincide with the annual Robert
Frost Birthday Celebration weekend; and the Short Story Workshop
in April. To request applications or more details on the creative
confabs, write to Key West
Writers Workshops, Heritage
House Museum, 410 Caroline
Street, Key West, Florida
33040; call (305) 296-3573;
or fax (305) 293-0482.

Perhaps Key West's most
outrageous celebration of the
written word is the week-long
spectacular known as the
Hemingway Days Festival.
This once-a-year literary
bacchanalia offers so much
that book nuts with a Mardi
Gras bent and exceptional
heat tolerance may want to

Royal Poinciana Tree

make reservations well in advance for the festivities which include
the Hemingway Look-Alike Contest; the Story-Telling Contest; the
Fish-Fry and Fish-Off; the Small Boat Regatta; Arm Wrestling
Championships; the Sunset Run; and the Radio Trivia Contest.

For the more literary-minded, look to the **Hemingway Days
Writers' Workshop and Conference**, a three-day program of round
tables, national speakers, and evening readings of poetry and fiction.
Past conferences have drawn such writers as John Updike, James

Dickey, Philip Caputo, George Plimpton, and numerous Hemingway scholars from around the country.

Hemingway family members take an active part in planning the conference and judging events. Writers Lorian Hemingway, the author's granddaughter; Hilary Hemingway, his niece; and her husband Jeffry Lindsay are instrumental in the First Novel Contest, the Short Story Competition, and the Young Writer's Scholarship Program. Staged during the week of Hemingway's birthday (July 21), two of the best functions are a "Meet the Writers" luncheon and the twilight birthday party and concert at the Hemingway House.

Founded in 1981, the festival has grown into an event-packed extravaganza with national sponsors. For applications to the literary conference and contests, write to Hemingway Days Festival, P.O. Box 4045, Key West, Florida 33041. To get more detailed information on any of the festivities, call festival director Michael Whalton at (305) 294-4440.

Equally eventful is the **Key West Theater Festival**. Launched to "nurture and inspire" new works for the stage, it succeeded beyond its grandest designs. In one year alone the theatrical fortnight has drawn 2,000 unproduced play manuscripts from around the world and staged nine debuts of original dramas. Sponsored by Key West's three nonprofit theaters (Red Barn Theatre, Waterfront Playhouse, and the Tennessee Williams Fine Arts Center), the dramatics marathon is in the skilled hands of artistic director Joan McGillis. For more on the two-week festival held each September, write: Key West Theater Festival, 1075 Duval Street, Key West, Florida 33040.

Watering Holes

Pilgrims to book shrines cannot live on legend alone. The following restaurant selections are among the Key West best. Wordsmithing is a hungry business. Sitting across a dining room from contemporary literary figures can only add spice to the plates at the table. Bon Appetit.

La Te Da, 1125 Duval Street. La Te Da is special. The white wood-fronted brick house leads to a small sprawl of hotel rooms that encircle a turquoise jewel of a pool. It is said that the Cuban patriot José Martí imbued a crowd with revolutionary fervor from the still-existing balcony. The house was termed La Terrazza de Martí—La Te Da.

Today, the flavor of revolution is still in evidence. For hotel rooms, dinner, or drinks after dark (and all day), La Te Da plays host to rebels of all stripe. Gays and straights, singers and swing-timers gather round Larry Smith's grand piano Thursday through Saturday nights. Chef Mary Wade's offerings under the fairy-lit trees beside the pool have, at this writing, a definite Italian accent. Fresh Key West shrimp is pesto-stuffed and wrapped in prosciutto. Shrimp again is paired with zucchini in a pancake and served with shaved parmesan and tomato-basil aioli. Local yellowtail becomes a piccata; sun-dried tomato ravioli is napped with roasted garlic cream. Do save room for pastry chef Sasha Van Cleef's sweet-tooth ticklers. John "Ma" Evans, probably the world's most dynamic social director, presides over Sunday afternoon tea dances and holiday parties. People still talk about the Easter weekend Ma turned the whole place into the Emerald City of Oz.

Antonia's, 615 Duval Street. Antonia's has always been popular with the writers-about-town. Tennessee Williams traditionally ordered red—Ruffino Ducale Reserve, one of the best Chiantis in the cellar. And the ever vibrant Italophile Leonard Bernstein became a genuine friend of the house. "Lenny," who thought that Antonia's truly felt like Italy, is described by the owners as "the dearest person we met through the restaurant."

At Antonia's, the food recalls the best Italian kitchens from SoHo to South Beach. The Milanese élan of maître d' Claudia Salvatore is difficult to find anywhere. Antonia Berto-Smith and Claudia Salvatore started the restaurant at the end of the 1970s when they came to the island from Italy. The authentic Italian influence shows up in the *gran gusto* of Chef Philip Smith's dishes. (Philip is Antonia's husband.) There's an understated chic to the place with its Dade County pine walls, original artworks, and clever use of ceiling canopies. One of the town's top restaurants, Antonia's is crowded most nights with a sophisticated mix of locals, snowbirds, and Europeans.

Starters to favor are the homemade mozzarella in the insalata caprese, the crostini assortimento, or the consistently divine soups. Half-orders of the wonderful housemade pastas also make an auspicious beginning to dinner. Malfatti—spinach-ricotta gnocchi— on a light tomato coulis are luscious as are the pesto lasagna and a classic linguine with small fresh clams in the shell.

Main courses such as lamb chops spiked with mustard and rosemary or the bundled-up fagottino of veal taste like the Italian countryside. Local fish fresh as the surrounding waters are done daily in different ways, and the stuffed chicken breast rollatini are light and lovely. The wine list, a thoughtful mix of Italy and California, is extremely well priced. Sweeter wines are offered by the glass to escort the kitchen's terrific desserts. Do indulge in a sip of the marvelous orange muscat, Quaddy Essentia.

The regular tables of the legends of the past are still filled by some very heavy-hitting writers. The soft-spoken Alison Lurie, who gave her legion fans *The Nowhere City* and *Foreign Affairs*, often runs into colleague and noted Pavarotti biographer, William Wright.

Sloppy Joe's Bar, 200 Duval Street. Who hasn't heard of Sloppy Joe's? Its reputation is worldwide as the two-fisted drinking man's hangout of Ernest Hemingway. Indeed, the macho writer's spirit breaks through the funk and grunge and noise. The seemingly always wide-open doors compel a walk-in to mingle in the mixed-up mixer hanging around the fight-scarred bar. Though the cuisine remains mostly sandwich fare—the Sloppy Joe being the most-ordered choice—Sloppy Joe's is never empty.

The legend of Papa Hemingway is alive and hanging on its walls. There's a spectacular mural starring the Old Man and some of his cronies. Uncashed royalty checks, the writer's birth certificate, and glossies of his sports conquests dot the cluttered surfaces. Today's clientele is a hodgepodge: black-leathered motorcycle

Sloppy Joe's Bar

jockeys; young, hell-raising spring breakers; old-time Conchs trying to drink themselves back to the past. Ernest Hemingway would have approved.

Pepe's Café, 806 Caroline Street. Pepe's is just the drop-in for some decidedly diverse dalliance. It's definitely a joint, albeit a hip one, with oversize wooden booths and a plain-as-hell outside garden. It's touted as being a Hemingway haunt. Just looking at Pepe's rustic trappings, one knows it would have been. Did Hemingway invent Pepe's? Or did Pepe's help to invent Hemingway?

The people at Pepe's claim to use only fresh fruit in their tropical drinks, but the main point at this bar is the spirits that are always hard and the Killian's on tap that is always ice-cold. Cold against the subtropical heat is a favorite theme with some of the old-timers at the picnic table out back. They love to wax on about the ice in the urinals—sophisticated civility in a he-man hangout.

A seeming vocation at Pepe's is to put meat—and plenty of it— on every meat-eater's bones. A few years ago, one of the touted specialties of this house was an enormous steak smothered in pork chops. *Carpe carnum.* Big steaks and thick pork chops are still on offer, though not necessarily together. Fish, too, flips onto an occasional plate, and raw Gulf oysters slip down copiously in cold, silvery swallows. Dinner is only one chapter of Pepe's three-part menu; breakfast and lunch are available there, too.

In March of 1994, Lawrence Ferlinghetti returned to the out- post island for the first time since 1943. It was "still Hemingway's Key West back then," opined the 75-year-old bard of the Beat Generation. During his visit he wrote *Three Key West Poems.* His *Poem #1* starts "Great breakfast at Pepe's ..." and ends with the poet imagining himself a camera and "fixing [the Pepe's scene] in the emulsion of my eternity." That's how one humble café joins the enviable terrain that makes up the "Coney Island" of Ferlinghetti's mind.

Café Marquesa, 600 Fleming Street. Cookbook-writer-in-residence Joe Famularo, whose recent *Celebrations* is a James Beard award winner, admits to having a preference for the Café Marquesa. He's not alone—the restaurant is a constant choice of Key West's literary colony. There's always a great likelihood that a table or two in the dining room will be peopled by well-known writers.

Who could blame them? The enchanting faux-painted café cozies into the front corner of The Marquesa, one of the best inns on the island. The always innovative kitchen is as modern as some of the scribes who sup there: garlic-dijon shrimp with sweet potato-andouille hash; fried oysters with yellow sun-dried tomato risotto and toasted ancho chili cream; grilled mahi-mahi with papaya-cucumber salsa and a black bean flan; cabernet-sauced black angus filet with potato quesadillas.

Louie's Backyard, 700 Waddell Avenue. And what a backyard it is—the Atlantic Ocean. It's a place to take your agent to ensure a terrific book sale. It's a place to have your publisher celebrate your million-dollar book advance.

But Louie's does not rest on its laurel-worthy geography alone. Lots of now-famous chefs have graduated from Louie's Backyard kitchen. All the influences at work in Key West have melded to form a sort of cuisine of the Caribbean Rim. The menu changes frequently, but Louie's stays immutable.

Square One, 1075 Duval Square. Square One on the upper reaches of Duval Street has a crisp, spit-and-polish look, so polished in fact that it seems to glow. Owner Michael Stewart defines the phrase "perfect host." Customers positively bask in his welcome. The barstool bonhomie is often chaired by Hemingway House guide and wit-about-town Larry Harvey. Harvey knows where everybody's bones are buried, and he is not shy about exhuming them. His repertoire of Capote capers and Hemingway high-jinks is worth a stop. So is the food.

The kitchen shines with its silky roasted garlic or snails in puff pastry as particularly appetizing appetizers. Grilled shrimp Square One and the plump scallops with lemon beurre blanc are perennial favorites. The grand piano background sounds of Joe Lowe and Paul Murray carry the crowd through dessert and digestifs.

Café des Artistes, 1007 Simonton Street. If other spots are super when a writer has just received a big advance, Café des Artistes is the place to go if he or she has just won a Pulitzer. This is arguably the finest restaurant in Key West.

Polished dark wood, bright white napery, and candleglow set an enticing stage for the knock-down brilliance of Chef Andrew Berman's Tropi-French cuisine. Housemade duck foie gras is satin on the tongue and a perfect partner to the bacon-vinaigrette wilted spinach. Roasted shrimps float like succulent islands in the stream of a pumpkin-spiked broth. Lobster, luxe enough on its own, is raised to new heights in a bath of passion fruit. This is food that inspires superlative prose.

Banana Café, 1211 Duval Street. Novelist turned occasional travel writer Joy Williams likes to trek through the menu of the Banana Café. The walls here are a trip, too, a virtual photo-library of Paris-gone-by. The Banana, named for the famed café in the Les Halles central market when it sat smack in the middle of Paris, is a true bistro. It tastes like France and has a feeling of the French Caribbean. The European charm of owners Christophe and Dani Collet and frontman Enzo Ursi make customers feel like they've taken a quick hop to the Continent. The prix-fixe is even priced in francs as well as dollars, and the food tastes simply delicious no matter what currency is used.

Further Reading

Brinnin, John Malcolm. *Truman Capote Dear Heart, Old Buddy.* New York: Dell Publishing Co., 1981.

Cox, Christopher. *A Key West Companion.* New York: St. Martin's Press, 1983.

Dodez, Lee. *Memories of Key West.* Key West: Lee Dodez, 1995.

Hersey, John. *Key West Tales.* New York: Alfred A. Knopf, 1994.

Humphrey, Mark and Harris Lewine. *Jimmy Buffett Scrapbook.* New York: Citadel Press, 1993.

Kaufelt, Lynn Mitsuko. *Key West Writers and Their Houses.* Sarasota: Pineapple Press, 1986.

McGuane, Thomas. *The Bushwhacked Piano.* New York: Simon & Schuster, 1971.

McLendon, James. *Papa: Hemingway in Key West.* Key West: Langley Press, Inc., 1990.

Murphy, George. *The Key West Reader.* Key West: Tortugas, Ltd., 1989.

Proby, Kathryn Hall. *Mario Sanchez: Painter of Key West Memories.* Key West: Southernmost Press, 1981.

Samuelson, Arnold. *With Hemingway: A Year in Key West and Cuba.* New York: Random House, 1984.

Sanchez, Thomas. *Mile Zero.* New York: Alfred A. Knopf, 1989.

Williams, Joy. *The Florida Keys.* New York: Random House, 1987.

Williams, Tennessee. *Memoirs.* New York: Doubleday & Company, Inc., 1975.

Windhorn, Stan and Wright Langley. *Yesterday's Key West.* Miami: Seemann Publishing Company, 1973.

Index